ALL RIGHTS RESERVED.

No part of this book may be reproduced or transmitted in any form or by any means, electronic or mechanical, including photocopying, recording, or by any information storage and retrieval system, without permission in writing from the author, except in the case of brief quotations embodied in reviews.

Cover Art: *Ollie and Esther Bliss*

Freedom

By Jane and Ryan Finch

Author's Note.

This is not a work of fiction.

Ryan age 4

Freedom

This is my son's story, but I am telling it because there are some things we sheltered him from, and so he was not aware of everything. He had enough to cope with. I will try not to sensationalise anything and just tell the facts. I'm not being over-emotional when I say that if I hadn't acted as I did, he may not be here today. Well, perhaps I am, but what parent wouldn't think that in the circumstances. There are so many stories in the news about young lives being taken because of despair and hopelessness and loss of self-esteem through bullying. It's time to be aware, and to take whatever action is necessary to protect your child.

Jane Finch

Foreword

I am delighted to have been asked to write a foreword for this important book on surviving bullying.

As founder and now president of Red Balloon Learner Centres I am always outraged by the stories I hear from children (and parents) of how their experiences of bullying have been disbelieved, ignored, or been dealt with badly.

I am humbled too by the determination, resilience and perseverance of parents whose children have been severely bullied and how they fight for the simple right of having a safe environment for their son or daughter to learn effectively. It is important to realise that the experience of bullying and the fact that it has not been recognised results in many of the children with whom Red Balloon deals developing social phobias, mental health problems and falling behind in their education. They need specialist help to recover.

I set up Red Balloon in my house with a friend, Ruth Loshak, in 1996 because of a child like Ryan. Parents whose daughter had attempted suicide as a result of bullying approached me. The thirteen-year-old had left her school and had been languishing at home for four months, becoming increasingly depressed and more intent on killing herself than previously. Her parents were beside themselves with worry, not only because their daughter was out of school and not getting an education, but also because her mental health was deteriorating.

I said, "Bring her to my house on Monday and I will see what I can do", totally unaware that this would change my life forever.

Nearly 18 years on Red Balloon now has four Centres, in Cambridge, Norwich, NW London and Reading, and a mini-Centre in Braintree, each taking about fifteen children. In addition we have launched a virtual Centre (Red Balloon of the Air) that can help a child anywhere in the UK.

Our aims have always been to:
1. Help restore the children's confidence, feeling of self-worth and self-esteem.
2. Get them back on an academic track.
3. Return them to mainstream education.

Over the last seventeen years we have helped nearly three hundred children.

If I had a wish it would be that heads, teachers and others would deal better with bullying in schools so that in a few years' time Red Balloon would no longer be needed. I fear my wish will not be granted.

Carrie Herbert MBE

Red Balloon Learner Centre Group

Freedom

CHAPTER ONE

'Will there be other children there?' Ryan asked as I fumbled with his duffle coat buttons and pulled the hood over his shiny curls.

'Oh yes,' I replied, 'and lots of new toys to play with. You'll really enjoy it.'

I scooped him up and strapped him into the buggy. I knew it would be pointless trying to get him to walk. I grabbed the dog, locked the door, and hurried down the driveway, yanking the dog away from the trees.

'Plenty of time to pee later, Buster'.

'Pee!' laughed Ryan.

The wheels of the buggy almost left the ground as I raced along the road. It was typical that we were going to be late on the first morning. I had wanted to line up with the other mothers so Ryan could be more prepared and I could see who was who. It was not going to be that way, though. As I skidded round the corner of the Church rooms I saw the last flowery skirt disappearing inside. The pathway was badly pitted and Ryan laughed as the buggy bounced and jumped along.

I tied the dog outside and lifted Ryan out, and with a deep breath opened the door. The mustiness of the place hit me at once. I couldn't help it but my nose wrinkled in disgust at the damp fetid smell. Why couldn't they find somewhere cleaner and healthier, I wondered.

Everyone turned in unison as we entered, and I closed the door behind me reluctantly, shutting out the crisp morning air. Ryan squiggled and I put him down on the floor. He sat and looked around him. The parents were warm and welcoming and smiled at Ryan as I struggled to undo his coat before he started exploring. Shirley introduced herself as the person in charge, and I completed the various forms and hurriedly signed my name.

'We like parents to stay a while for the first few visits,' she announced, so I nodded and found a seat, hoping the dog would not get too cold outside. I thought I could probably spare a few minutes before racing home again and getting ready for work. Good job I didn't start until 10am. It just meant that Buster's walk would have to wait.

Ryan was clingy and reluctant to release his grip on my knees. There was lots of laughter and chatter from the other children and I took him over to a little group and let him watch them for a while. There was a climbing frame as well but I didn't take him near that. He was very prone to falling off things and didn't seem to have a very tight grip and I didn't want him to fall and hurt himself on his first visit. So far at home he had hit himself with the swing and fallen off the slide so many times we had packed them both up and put them in the shed.

Another child had begun to show Ryan how to put plastic rings on to a holder and Shirley sidled up to me.

'Now might be a good time to sneak out,' she whispered, so I gathered up my things and walked backwards towards the door. Ryan didn't appear to notice, so I slid quietly outside to be greeted by a very relieved dog who doubtless thought he had been abandoned.

I listened for a few minutes. I could hear Ryan because he spoke quite loudly and didn't form his words well so I could tell his voice apart from the others. I peered through the window and he was still playing with the rings. So I left.

The dog and I hurried home, poor Buster hopping on three legs as he tried to christen every tree we passed. I gave him a hug and some breakfast and dashed off to work.

Two hours later as I parked outside the Church I heard Ryan screaming. Shirley saw me coming and stopped me before I went inside.

'Look,' she said 'there's been a bit of an incident, but it's nothing to worry about.'

'What incident? What's wrong?'

She put her hand on my shoulder as she explained what had happened.

'The children were getting excited as the mothers started to arrive. Ryan was looking for you – well you were a bit late – and …well….'

'Well what?'

Shirley drew a circle on her cheek.

'Ryan has been bitten.'

'Bitten?' I repeated, having so many questions but feeling stupidly lost for words. 'How did it happen?'

I tried to keep calm as she explained how Ryan had become more and more anxious as parents arrived and I was not there. He started to cry and another child hit him. When he didn't stop, the child bit him. Somehow she made it seem like it was my fault for being late. When I showed her my watch and said in fact I was exactly on time, she then staggered me by saying,

'Well Ryan is so placid, he should have hit back, and then he wouldn't have been bitten. They've got to learn to stand up for themselves at an early age, you know.'

'Are you saying..' I spluttered '….that Ryan got bitten because he would not fight?'

She began to nod, and then stopped herself, seeing that I was clearly furious.

'Look, take him home now and put a cold compress on his face. I'm sure he'll get used to everyone soon.'

Ryan cried all the way home, and his cheek was red and swollen. The teeth marks were clearly visible. I hugged him and called him my best boy and wondered how I was going to get him to nursery the next day.

CHAPTER TWO

Melanie was explaining about the job, doing her best to persuade me it was a good idea to have a complete career change.

'You're always saying you've had enough of law,' she said,' well here's your chance to get out of it.'

I read through the details again. Manager of a retirement complex. It just didn't seem like my type of thing and I said so but Melanie waved my concerns away.

'You might just enjoy it.'

So it wasn't long afterwards that we were packing up and moving to a new town and a new job. It was January 1998, and heavy snow was forecast so we were hoping to get moved in before the roads became blocked as was always the case when snow fell in Norfolk. We all got up bright and early on moving day, planning an early start. Melanie arrived on schedule to collect Ryan and keep him amused at her house.

'So you'll bring him over this evening?'

'Don't worry, just concentrate on moving boxes and I'll see you later.' Ryan went off quite happily. Melanie was his godmother, after all and she had been a part of his life since he was born. Often I referred to her as his fairy godmother.

The village seemed a nice place. There was a large grassed area a bit like a park, where people walked their dogs and children played football and toddlers screamed and giggled without bothering anyone. There was a little pond which we had been told teemed with tadpoles in the spring. In January it was frozen solid, but it looked somewhere full of promise for a youngster with a fishing net and vivid imagination. We were early, so stopped in the early morning frost and watched the dog walkers.

'I hope we've made the right decision,' I said, and my husband Chris took my hand reassuringly.

'It'll be alright', he whispered. His illness had started when Ryan was born, and so he was hoping that this might be a fresh start where no-one knew about his condition and there would be no awkward questions.

'Let's go and see if we can pick up the keys yet,' he said. 'We want to get the place as organized as possible before Ryan arrives.'

+++

One day was all I had to unpack, and then I had to start my new job. It was also Ryan's first day at primary school, and he was struggling to get into his uniform. His jumper was backwards and his socks were inside out. I tried to keep calm and not keep looking at my watch.

'Come on, my best boy,' I said, 'let's get you sorted out,' and Ryan stood as I straightened his clothes and tied his laces. Chris was going to walk to the school with us. He could probably have taken Ryan on his own, but I wanted to be there for his first day, and to meet the teacher.

As usual Ryan was reluctant to walk but we played his favourite game of run and catch up and it worked a treat.

'It does worry me that he can't dress himself yet,' I whispered to Chris as we walked, 'and I don't think he will ever be able to tie those laces.'

'Stop worrying.'

'Well, you see other kids his age and they seem to have no problem.'

We had caught Ryan up by then and reached the school gates. I took his hand and we all walked into the reception class and I introduced him to the teacher. She was homely and had a kind face and I took to her straight away.

'Of course,' she began, 'the other children all know each other and have formed their friendships already because they have been here for a term,' she looked at Ryan and ruffled his hair, 'but I'm sure Ryan will soon fit in.'

She began to shuffle us towards the door.

'Off you go,' she urged, 'he'll be fine.'

After that the day was a blur. When I arrived at the complex most of the eighty residents had turned out to meet me. I think they were just as curious about me as I was about them. Ryan seemed happy and tired when I went home, so I breathed a sigh of relief.

+++

Three days later, and I was taking a short coffee break, telling Chris about some of the comical traits of the senior citizens I was looking after, when the telephone rang.

'It's the First School, could you arrange to call in some time today?'

'Is there a problem?' I asked, frantically wondering how I was going to get any time off work during my first week.

'We'd rather discuss it with you in person.'

I was mystified. What was so urgent and complicated that it could not be dealt with on the telephone and why was it so important that I had to take time off work?

Strictly speaking, I was on call all day and couldn't leave the site. Chris could have gone, but I wanted to know first hand what the problem was, so I handed over to emergency call at lunchtime and hurried down to the school.

The teacher who I had thought was homely and kind looked grim and stern.

'Ryan has major problems,' she declared. 'He doesn't listen to instructions, he drops things, he won't do as he is told, and he doesn't pay attention.'

I could feel my face getting hot.

'He's only four,' I replied, struggling to remain calm.

'Well he's disrupting the class. I want you to take him home every lunchtime for the foreseeable future until he settles in.'

'He's not going to settle in very quickly if he's only here for half a day at a time'.

'Mrs. Finch, please do not argue with me. We are the experts and we come across this sort of thing all the time.'

'What sort of thing?' I asked, really curious as to what she thought this 'thing' was, but she dismissed me with a flick of her hand.

'Twelve o'clock every day. Make sure you collect him promptly, please.'

Later I would think of all sorts of retorts, but for that moment I sat in stunned silence. How was I going to juggle this? What if Chris had a bad day and couldn't take care of Ryan?

CHAPTER THREE

Life was really difficult. Work was demanding and the days that Chris was unwell meant I needed to keep checking at home to make sure he was coping alright with Ryan. I decided to telephone the school and see just how much longer they deemed Ryan had to be restricted to half days.

'It's funny you should call today, Mrs. Finch, because we've just heard that the school psychologist is coming to see Ryan tomorrow.'

'Psychologist?' I could hear my voice rising. 'Why have you called a psychologist?'

'It's normal practice, Mrs. Finch, when we suspect that a child has special needs.'

This was getting quite bizarre. Not only were they saying Ryan was having problems adjusting to school but now he had special needs and they had called in a psychologist.

'Was anyone going to consult me?' I asked.

'Certainly, we were about to call you…'

I sighed. I was obviously getting nowhere.

'What time tomorrow?' Yet another occasion when I needed to take time off work. Still, perhaps it would result in Ryan returning to full-time schooling and he might have more opportunity to settle.

The following day I sat in a side office with Ryan and the smiling psychologist. She was very nice, and explained to me what she intended to do.

'I just have a few little written exercises I'd like Ryan to do, and then some pictures to look at.'

I sat back and watched as Ryan was shown flash cards, asked to draw various shapes, and asked to explain a variety of images. As I was watching I noticed that the psychologist was talking very slowly and leaning towards him. She was pointing at many of the images and it seemed to me that Ryan was listening and responding to her very well. Eventually he went back to his class and she turned to me and I tensed as I waited for her to give me her verdict.

'Well, it's fairly clear that Ryan has Asperger's Syndrome.'

'What was that?' She spelt it as I wrote it down.

'What is it,' I asked, 'I've never heard of it.'

'I'll send you some information in the post. It's a form of autism.'

I fell back in my chair with a thud. I couldn't think of anything to say, I was just astounded. Ryan was fine at home, well behaved, and responsive. There was no doubt there were problems at school, but autism? Just like that?

She patted my hand.

'Don't get upset, dear, there's lots of help available. We'll get him registered as special needs and then get him some help in school. Then he'll be able to come back full time, which is what you want, isn't it?'

The pack of information arrived a few days later, and I could feel my blood pressure rising as I read through details of symptoms, diagnosis, prognosis and resources available. I reached for the telephone and dialed the number for the school's liaison officer. I explained who I was and why I was calling.

'Ryan has very few of these symptoms. I agree he doesn't mix well and tends to play on his own, but none of the other symptoms fit.'

'Parents often find it difficult to accept a diagnosis of Asperger's Syndrome. I would suggest you read through the information carefully and take time to absorb it all. Let's speak again in a week or two.'

I was so staggered I could not respond properly. I just hung up the telephone and stared at it. I looked across the room at Ryan. He was laying on the floor looking at his favourite book, swinging his legs in the air and looking perfectly content as he chatted to himself. I called him softly.

'Ryan'.

No answer. I called him again. Still no response. I moved a bit closer.

'Ryan'.

He still carried on looking at his book, acting as if he had not heard me. I tried a different approach.

'Anyone want something to eat?'

It definitely seemed like he did not hear me. I moved closer still and touched his arm,

'Would you like something to eat?'

He jumped up immediately.

'Yes please. Biscuit?'

It was then that a possibility hit me. Maybe he had a hearing problem. That would explain his not interacting well with peers, and his failure to respond to instructions in the classroom. I headed for the telephone again to call the doctors and arrange an appointment for a hearing test.

+++

'Can you turn the television down?' asked Ryan, and that was when I knew that the operation to put gromits in his ears had been successful. Already the school was beginning to be more positive, saying that he was paying attention in class and responding to instructions.

CHAPTER FOUR

So now I needed to address what the school referred to as his clumsiness, but I saw it as a lack of co-ordination. I thought that practice would make perfect so arranged for him to join the football training on a Saturday morning.

It was pouring with rain, but the teams met whatever the weather, so I dressed Ryan in his shorts and top and new football socks and boots, and off we went. He was very excited and began warming up with the others. It seemed things were going well, he was stretching and jogging and managing to keep up. Then they brought out the balls and the boys were told to practice dribbling skills and pick-ups. Ryan found this totally impossible and had no control over the ball at all. At first the others tried to help him, but they soon began to tease him and then to make fun of his attempts to kick the ball.

'Behind you, Ryan.'

'Hey, over here.'

'Why don't you just pick it up and carry it?'

Other parents were laughing, and I couldn't believe they were joining in with their children in ridiculing Ryan. I glared at them, to no avail. I could see that he was trying really hard, but it was like the ball had a weight inside it and rolled away from him whenever he went near it.

'Run for the ball, Ryan, run for it,' shouted the coach, and Ryan did his best but the others raced past him and his legs tangled up and down he went, to a chorus of laughter from the sidelines.

All this time and the rain was falling in sheets. We returned home in silence and I gave him a hot bath.

'Will I get better?' he asked, and my heart went out to him. I knew how much he wanted to fit in and be a part of the sporty crowd.

'Give it a few weeks,' I said, 'and I'm sure you'll be fine.'

I tried to focus on his strengths, and so we tried a number of social activities. Twice a week I took him to judo classes in a town a few miles away, hoping that the discipline of the sport would help him with his co-ordination, but I could see after a while that he was not enjoying it. Simple things like how to hold an opponent which seemed easy to others was complicated and frustrating for Ryan.

Swimming lessons were more successful, and I was surprised he took to it so well. At first it was a disaster with an instructor who didn't understand his reluctance to enter the water and tipped him in when he hesitated to jump in. I was not pleased, as this had the effect of making him frightened of the water. However, we persisted with a new instructor and eventually Ryan was able to co-ordinate his arms and legs and swim quite well. What he did have was upper body strength which meant he could move through the water quickly and swiftly, even if the strokes might not be quite right. However, the fact that he could hold his own in the water with the other children was good for his confidence.

He was so eager to gain praise from the other children that he put every ounce of strength and effort into the swimming. At one particular session I could see he was struggling and told him to stop and rest, but he was determined to be as good as the others. The better swimmers were doing laps and Ryan was keeping up with them, although he was finally starting to slow down.

'Anybody who has had enough can stop now, you've all done really well,' called the swimming instructor. Ryan looked around and although a few stopped, others carried on, so he did too. He was getting really slow, and then he drifted to the side and stayed there. I could stand it no longer and rushed over and helped him out of the pool. He was so weak he couldn't stand. I wrapped him in a towel and took him outside to get some air, and he began vomiting. He had given every ounce of strength he possessed to try and keep up with the other swimmers.

'Did I do good?' he asked. I gave him a huge hug and told him he had been brilliant.

CHAPTER FIVE

Once again I decided I needed to take things into my own hands to find out why Ryan had difficulty in simple things like tying shoelaces, catching a ball, or carrying a plate without everything falling off it. I wasn't prepared to accept that this was just down to clumsiness. Watching him at the football sessions had convinced me that as hard as he might try, Ryan could just not co-ordinate his movements easily.

I didn't really know where to start, as I thought these things were supposed to be dealt with by the school, so I thumbed through the telephone directory until I came across children's services, and dialed their number.

'I'd just like some advice,' I began, explaining about Ryan's lack of co-ordination and difficulties in practical things.

'Why don't you have him assessed?' the lady suggested, and she gave me the details of how to do this.

So we found ourselves at a child assessment centre, and Ryan began to go through a series of tests. He had to walk in a straight line, balance on his toes, draw a circle, read some words from a picture book, talk about the pictures, and a variety of other little games that were designed to assess his fine motor skills.

At the end of the assessment Ryan was talking to another assistant whilst the assessor spoke to me.

'I'd like to refer him for a firm diagnosis, but I think Ryan has dyspraxia.'

She saw my confused look, and began to explain.

'Dyspraxia used to be known as Clumsy Child Syndrome. It is a condition that affects the planning and carrying out of an action. The messages to the brain are not properly transmitted. It affects the organization of movement. I can see that Ryan has difficulty in holding a pencil and standing on his tiptoes. The other tests show this is probably why Ryan is finding activities hard.'

I felt a tremendous relief because there was finally a reason why Ryan found simple tasks so challenging.

Once I had the combined diagnosis of hearing loss and dyspraxia I was able to show the school and the various psychologists that had seen Ryan that he did not have any special needs. It took a total of three years arguing with the authorities before it was conceded that Ryan did not have Asperger's nor any form of autism. It took yet another year before his name was removed from the special needs list and again I had to insist that the reference was removed from his school records.

It wasn't that I didn't want Ryan labelled with a condition such as Asperger's, but that I didn't want him wrongly diagnosed, because it would be something that would follow him throughout his life, so it needed to be a firm diagnosis, and there were too many variables and possibilities. There were too many references in the psychologists reports to 'similar to' and 'could be' and 'possibility of' and I pushed and pushed until further tests were carried out and I found out exactly what was going on.

Finally, I received that hard-fought notification. My hand was shaking as I re-read the letter from the school.

'Dear Mrs. Finch, this is to confirm that Ryan's name has now been removed from the special needs register and all references to his having Asperger's Syndrome have been removed from his records.'

CHAPTER SIX

When Ryan was seven he began suffering from sickness and unexplained illnesses.

'My tummy hurts.'

He came and sat on my lap and buried his head in my sweater.

'I think I'd better stay at home tomorrow.'

I gave him a big hug.

'I'm sure you will feel better in the morning,' I said, but he huddled even closer and groaned.

'It hurts.'

'Let's watch a cartoon together, and I bet it goes away.'

But it didn't, and soon the nightly vomiting began. It was a while before I realised that these only occurred during the week, and the symptoms disappeared at weekends. I tried not to worry too much and attempted to take his mind off school in the evenings. For a few hours he would be better, but then by the time he went to bed the sickness started again. I began to get suspicious that all was not well at school, but he refused to talk about it.

One day there was a gentle knock at the door. I answered to find two little children from the school. One of them was very nervous and fiddling with her sleeve.

'Are you Ryan's mum?' she asked.

'Yes. Did you want to see Ryan?' I hoped so. He never had friends call for him. Perhaps they had been playing at school.

'We just thought you ought to know that Ryan's getting hit a lot. In the playground.'

The other child nodded.

'And kicked.'

'We thought you should know.'

I thanked them for telling me and asked if they knew who was hitting him.

'Two of the older boys.'

I decided to see for myself, and the next day I went to the school entrance and watched as the children came out to play. It wasn't long before I saw Ryan pinned against the fence and being pummelled by two boys. I shouted at them.

'Hey you two, what are you doing?' and they saw me and ran away. Ryan just huddled into the fence and I had the awful feeling that this was a regular occurrence, just like the children had told me. I found myself in the head teacher's office and listened to her tell me adamantly that there was absolutely no bullying at her school.

'But I saw it with my own eyes. Two children came to the house and told me what was happening. They were upset.'

'Mrs. Finch, I can tell you categorically there is no bullying in this school. I do not allow it. We have very strict policies in place.'

The next day I turned up again at playtime, but this time went into the school and asked the head teacher to accompany me. We walked into the playground together and we saw Ryan standing alone.

'He seems fine,' she began, and then be both watched as two boys went up to Ryan and began to push him. He turned away from them but they pushed him in the back and he fell over. They began to kick him as he curled into a ball on the floor. I couldn't watch any more and hurried over, the head teacher following close behind. The huge grins on the boys' faces quickly disappeared as she marched them back into the school, and I helped Ryan up and brushed the dirt from his clothes.

'Come on, Ryan,' I said, 'we're going home,' and we just walked out. I telephoned the head teacher when I got home and told her Ryan was not coming back until I was sure she could protect him.

I received a letter of apology from her, admitting that Ryan had been bullied. Ryan then told me that this happened all the time. He had been afraid to talk about it because he thought that telling would make things worse. I hugged him hard and told him that the teachers were now aware and they would keep and eye on him and protect him.

The question in my mind was why he was being subjected to bullying. He was a quiet boy, not a fighter, he never argued, and had done nothing to cause the boys to pick on him.

What became apparent over a period of time was that Ryan's dyspraxia actually had quite an effect on his socialising. Dyspraxia makes co-ordination difficult, with the result that he was never any good at sports, although he tried really hard. He could not catch, could not kick a ball and make it go where it was supposed to go, and his running was awkward and slow. This meant that he became the butt of jokes and jibes. I think that was how it started.

I dreaded sports days. Parents were so passionate about winning, but I just wanted Ryan to finish the race. I always remembered how my parents had never been to my sports days when I was at school. Every time I looked for them, but they never came. So I was determined to support Ryan, encourage him, praise him, and focus on his successes. I could never quite understand the teacher's logic. Of course, all sports were compulsory, so he had to run in the relays, and no-one wanted him on their team. He was always the last choice. I could see how hard he was trying, but his arms would flail and his legs would tangle and more often than not he ended up on the floor. I glared at other parents when they laughed at him. I spoke to the sports teacher and suggested that they could let Ryan help in other ways such as setting out the equipment, but that was not the way things were done, and it was set in stone. They would put him in goal, for instance, when they knew he could not catch. It seemed to me they set him up to fail.

The weekday illnesses continued. I constantly telephoned the school to ask if anything was going on. Was Ryan alright in classes, were they keeping an eye on him in the playground, was his work suffering in any way? The doctor had dismissed the constant sickness as attention-seeking, but I decided to get another opinion. The stomach aches and the vomiting were very real and I felt they must be having a detrimental affect on his overall health. The second doctor took a completely different view. He showed concern for Ryan, spending time talking to him, expressing his concern to me. Things were happening that were making Ryan ill and it needed to be dealt with. He decided to write to the school to alert them of his concerns.

It was heartbreaking each morning, trying not to be concerned with the vomiting, the reluctance to get dressed, and hanging back the nearer we got to the school gates. He still refused to talk about what was worrying him, and I tried not to push the questions. I tried to encourage Ryan, expressing excitement about various events at school, and really praising him when he won a star for effort or for a piece of work. It was difficult, though, because everything was geared around sports. It was football, or races, or basketball, or rounders. There didn't seem to be any outside activities for someone who couldn't catch. It was so hard, watching him trying to play a game with a ball. He would follow it with his eyes, his face would look determined, he would move back to position himself and hold out his hands, and then the ball would pass straight through his hands like there was a giant hole in them.

When the time at Middle School ended, it was a great relief to the whole family. Ryan began to relax and enjoy himself again, and the ritual of sickness and illness ceased. We enjoyed the summer and I thought we had turned a corner. Towards September I bought the new uniform for High School, and Ryan paraded for photographs, proud in his new outfit.

'It looks really cool, Ryan, and it suits you.'

He was pleased, and so excited the first morning of starting High School, he barely slept the night before. I was so happy for him, and there were tears in my eyes as I watched him leave to catch the school bus. He had such a big grin on his face and I longed to give him a huge hug and just hold on to him. I so wanted to protect him and I thought about him all day, wondering how he would be getting on, and hoping and praying that he was finally enjoying school.

At four o'clock the telephone rang.

'Mum, I'm at nan's. I'm going to stay here. Can you come and get me?'

My mother's house was next to the drop off point for the bus. Confused, I hurried there, to find that his face and head were red and swollen. Huge tears were falling down his face. He sat with a cold flannel against his forehead.

'What happened? Did you fall?' I asked. He shook his head.

My mother was looking grim.

'They hit him,' she said, 'on the bus.'

I looked at my son and saw the hurt in his eyes. He had been so excited when he had left that morning, with such expectations and anticipation. I put my arm around him.

'Tell me what happened.'

He sniffed as the tears began to fall again.

'I was just sitting on the seat when someone leant over from behind and punched me in the head.'

His sobbing grew louder and I looked up and saw the angry look on my mother's face.

'Then someone else started hitting me, slapping my face, kicking me. They took my school bag and tipped everything onto the floor and then stood on my books.'

I just listened, seeing it all in my mind.

'They were all laughing. It was horrible.'

'Do you know who it was?' I asked.

He nodded and gave me their names. One of the boys lived next door to us.

I took Ryan home and as soon as he was settled watching a cartoon I went round to see the boy next door and to speak to his parents. I told his mother what had happened and I could see him standing behind her, smirking. I looked over to him.

'Why would you do that to him?' I asked. He glared at me and shrugged his shoulders.

'Don't you realize how important today was to him? Do you remember what it was like on your first day at High School?'

Again, he just shrugged. His mother looked helpless. Clearly this wasn't getting me anywhere.

'You do realize I can report this to the Police? You have assaulted and injured my son.'

That got his attention. He told me he was sorry and would come and apologise to Ryan. He came round and shook Ryan's hand and said he was sorry and wouldn't do it again. He called him his 'mate'. I almost believed him.

One thing that had passed through my mind briefly was that the kids who had been a problem at primary school and through middle school were a year older, and they would be at the High School. I had hoped, however, that they would have forgotten about Ryan. Unfortunately, they had not, and they now had a gang.

My heart was broken yet again. I had seen him so proud and expectant and excited in his new uniform, a new school and new people. His first day, and the gang of bullies had found him. Worse than that, the gang leader lived next door.

I rang the school but was told the head teacher was too busy to speak to me. I made an appointment for the following day, and took Ryan along with me so that she could see his injuries.

Even though I had an appointment, I was told she was still too busy to speak to me. I saw the deputy head and explained what had happened. I asked if there was any supervision on the bus. There was not. I asked if as a parent I could travel on the bus, and perhaps set up a rota with other parents. This was not allowed for insurance reasons, I was advised. What did they have to offer to ensure my son's safety, I asked. The deputy shrugged his shoulders and said Ryan must have provoked them.

After that I took Ryan to school each day by car, so at least I knew he would have a stress-free journey to start his day. But I knew things were not right. As I pulled into the car park he would give me such a heart-rending look, then reluctantly get out of the car and I would watch as he took a quick look around and hurried to his classroom. I would stay and watch until he was out of sight.

One day I saw a group of boys following him, nudging each other and laughing. I decided I had seen enough and went into the school office. Again the head teacher was too busy to talk to me so I saw another teacher.

'Is there anywhere he can go at breaks?' I asked. He saw I was upset and I explained what had been happening and how I had just seen some boys following Ryan. I said if I was going to bring him to school I needed to know he was safe.

'Tell him he can go to classroom B2 at any time. That's the IT centre, and it's always open.'

Armed with this information I told Ryan and for a few days he seemed a little brighter. Then I noticed bruises on his legs.

'How did you get those?' I asked.

He shrugged his shoulders.

'Come on, Ryan. What happened?'

Then he told me how for a couple of days things were alright and he would go into the IT room at lunchtime and breaks, but then the boy from next door had seen him and followed him in. Then others arrived, and then that was that and they started tormenting him. It was so sad to see him drained of enthusiasm. His excitement had gone, he was silent and withdrawn, talking little about his day or the school. He wouldn't go outside, not even in the back garden, but sat in the back room just watching television, huddled up and silent. Then he started vomiting again.

CHAPTER SEVEN

I understand how difficult it can be to relate or sympathise with bullying if you have never experienced it or been a victim. At school I was well up with the top performers academically and so was well respected. I had a good circle of friends and although I never reached my goal of Head Girl, I was a prefect and I carried out those duties diligently. Looking back now I can remember many times in my prefect role when I would break up fights and skirmishes. At the time I dismissed them as insignificant, but with hindsight I can identify bullying. The victim was often the same boy or girl, and they would have few or no friends and would be quiet and withdrawn in the classroom. Often I would find them cowering in a cupboard and just send them outside to join everyone else. Now I can see I was sending them into the den of wolves. Some of them would disappear from school altogether and I never gave it a thought.

So I don't condemn or judge anyone who does not empathise with those who have been bullied, because until it touches you personally there is probably no reason why anyone should.

There are extremes, though. So many times I have heard or read the comment that those who claim to be bullied should toughen up and take it on the chin, giving as good as they get. But what about those who don't have the time to toughen up, or it's just not in their nature?

For Ryan, the intimidation started when he was three. From the time he started to mix with other children he was singled out, so from an early age he began to protect himself by putting up barriers. This was in the way of withdrawing from the crowd and playing on his own. At the time I had no idea what was going on within him, I just felt sad for him that he always seemed to be alone, and that was how it continued.

A couple of months after Ryan had started at High School I heard a local radio report about a group that was starting up in the area. There was to be a meeting for the parents of children who were being bullied. The organisation was called Red Balloon. I received several text messages from friends and family who had also heard the story, and they urged me to attend. I didn't really know what to expect, but decided to go along. There were several families, married couples and single parents, all looking tired and drawn and worried. It was suggested that to break the ice we all gave our stories of why we were there. What I heard that day will stay with me always.

The first couple told about their daughter who had been bullied because of the way she looked. She had tried to take her life on several occasions and was currently hospitalised and on suicide watch. Others told of their children who wouldn't come out of their rooms, who couldn't hold eye contact, and whose self esteem was so low they would not look in a mirror. It was only during this meeting that I realised just how serious a problem bullying can be. We all cried as we heard each other's stories, and as I listened I found out that Ryan was the only child who remained at school. Everyone else had removed their child from the state system either for their emotional or physical wellbeing, or both.

We agreed to meet again the following week, and to bring our children along as well. For me this was quite a big decision, because it meant I would have to take Ryan out of school for the day, and I would have to explain to the school why I was doing so. It also meant that I was on the way to admitting that we had a serious problem to deal with.

At the next meeting the children sat round a large table. Ryan had been delighted to get away from school for a day and had willingly agreed to attend the meeting. He still refused to talk about what happened at school, and I hoped being with other kids who had experienced similar bullying might enable him to be more open about how he was feeling. I left the room briefly as the children were getting settled, and it was only on my return that I began to see what was happening to my son. As the other children had entered the room, he had begun to curl up in his seat, dropping his head and avoiding eye contact with anyone. I was horrified to see him like that, but the counsellors there understood, and gently tried to include him in the conversations.

The parents stood at the back of the room as the counsellors began to introduce themselves. There was no condemnation of Ryan's stance, no shout to straighten up and pay attention. He was not singled out for most of the others were also sitting with their eyes lowered and their shoulders sagging. I had to leave the room because I was crying so much, and I didn't want Ryan to see. One of the counsellors followed me out, and explained that Ryan was in defensive mode, protecting himself from an expected onslaught of either verbal or physical abuse. I cried even more.

After that Ryan went once a week, and he looked forward to it. He had one-to-one sessions with a counsellor and I was told he was beginning to open up, although I wasn't given any details. Everything was confidential and it was up to Ryan if he chose to share with me what was said. It was very difficult to know that my son was talking about his problems to someone else but I tried really hard to see this as a positive and not to push him into talking to me until he was ready.

A few weeks later the group decided to meet twice a week, but I explained that the school would not let Ryan have any more time off and he would have to stick to one session a week. It was on the way home from that meeting that Ryan began to cry. I pulled the car into a layby, put my arm around him, and waited. It seemed to me that something quite profound was happening, and that he was actually reached a crisis of some sort. It was a very emotional time and we cried our hearts out together. I hugged him and told him he was my best boy. After a while when he had calmed down, Ryan begged me to let him go to the group twice a week. He said that he had no worries whilst he was there. When I asked what sort of worries, he said he didn't have to think about the others laughing at him, or picking on him, or singling him out and making fun of him. Apart from home he said it was the one place where he felt he could be free. That was a statement that really hit me. What was going on and why did he see the centre as freeing him. He told me he really wanted to go there as much as possible. In fact, he went further than that. He told me he wanted to leave school and that he couldn't bear it any longer. He was finally opening up to me. As the traffic raced past, he told me what his days were like.

    I heard how he would hurry from one classroom to another to avoid being caught by the other boys, who would trip him up, or push him over, punch him, or steal his bag, at every opportunity. If the classroom was locked, as was often the case, he would hide under stairwells or in remote corridors. He told me how he hid at lunchtimes and couldn't eat much of his lunch because he was so scared, and how he couldn't concentrate on lessons because of missiles that were thrown at him, rude notes sent to him, and his work book scrawled on. He was kicked and punched and slapped and poked constantly. His daily life consisted of running and hiding and watching his back. "I'm so tired of running," he told me. I promised that we would all talk about it as a family that evening.

My husband was reluctant to agree to take Ryan out of school. He felt that school was something that was necessary and essential and that it would be socially unacceptable for a child not to attend school. He tried to teach Ryan how to fight, and told him every time someone hit him to hit back. But it was soon clear that because of his dyspraxia Ryan did not have the co-ordination to punch properly. My husband could see that if Ryan ever showed any retaliation he would be beaten really badly. The other aspect is that Ryan is really placid and gentle, and he didn't have it in him to try to hurt anyone. I know this may sound like an over-protective parent seeing her son through rose-coloured glasses, but that is truly how he is.

The group at Red Balloon had spoken about other options being available, such as home schooling, but I had no idea how I could please my husband by providing a structured learning schedule as well as educate Ryan to the standard of GCSE. So we compromised, and it was agreed that Ryan would go twice weekly to the group, but continue at school for the remainder of the time. This would be a trial, and we would see how things went.

When I told the school of our decision they said I was neglecting Ryan's education and did not have his best interests at heart. I was advised I would be reported to the authorities as I was damaging my son's future prospects and his emotional well being. This was very worrying, almost like blackmail, and I wondered if I was doing the right thing. It was only after discussion with the group members and the counsellors that I realised it was not a legal requirement to send a child to school. As long as some system of learning was in place, then there was nothing anyone could do. It might not be socially acceptable, but it was not illegal.

So I began to research home schooling. I joined Education Otherwise and spoke to other parents who had been home educating their children. Some had taken their children out of school because of bullying, some because of their discontent with the educational system such as the size of classes, and some had never sent their children to school at all. One parent might have a completely different idea of education than another. For example, some would focus on their child's strengths and interests, such as art and creativity, whilst others chose to let their children elect what they learnt and how. I knew that if I was ever to persuade my husband to agree to Ryan leaving school permanently I would have to put in place a structured learning programme and schedule and there would have to be an ultimate goal, that is, GCSE's.

I didn't really know what Ryan's academic ability was, because he had never been free to develop his interests at school. The Red Balloon group was beginning to develop and expand, bringing in tutors to help with basics such as maths and science. They told me Ryan was outstanding at maths, and had some creativity in writing. Gradually I could seem him beginning to relax both when interacting with the other children, and with his learning. He started to write stories at home, something he had never done before. He began to read more and was even excited when given maths homework to do. The two meetings a week helped Ryan to get through his weeks at school, but I knew he was still struggling. I could see it in his eyes when he left for school each morning. Just getting out of the car took tremendous effort, and he would look quickly around and then dash for his classroom. I found myself staying in the car park longer and longer each day, watching the other boys to see if anyone was going to follow him. If it affected me like that, then I couldn't even begin to understand how Ryan was feeling.

I tried to focus on his self-esteem, arranging for him to have braces fitted to his teeth which protruded slightly, and doing away with his spectacles and having contact lenses. I died his hair and had it styled, and went to more expensive stores and encouraged him to choose stylish clothes. The school told me that it was not his outward appearance that was the problem, but his lack of social skills. They refused to accept that it was because he constantly felt threatened and intimidated. I tried to explain what I had learnt from the Red Balloon counsellors, that he was being defensive and was afraid to socialise with his peers because of what was happening. I did feel that some progress was being made, though, with the regular group meetings. Ryan had developed a real rapport with his counsellor, and he was now talking to me about his problems at school. I started to understand what it must be like to be ostracised by everyone and to live a solitary existence, always afraid someone was going to jump out at you and give you a beating. Such a youngster and living in fear. It just didn't seem fair.

And then it was Halloween.

CHAPTER EIGHT

As Christians, we did not believe in participating in Halloween, but we had always allowed Ryan to give out sweets to the young children that dressed up and came calling with their smiling parents. One year, however, things took a sinister turn. Ryan was still too scared to go out of the house by himself, so I knew that the gang from the school were still targeting him. It was a problem that they lived so near which was why we always ensured that either myself or my husband were with him when he was out.

On this particular 31st October, Ryan was waiting with the basket of sweets. When there was a knock on the door he answered it alone, and I heard him yell. I ran to the door to see a couple of boys had knocked the basket from his hands, pulled him outside, and had him pinned against the side of our car. I shouted at them, and they ran away. A short time later there was another knock, and I went behind Ryan, so that I could not be seen from the doorway but I could see who was there. The same two boys stood at the door and snatched the basket away from him. They went to pull him outside and

I stepped forward to see a group of about six other boys hiding behind the open door. I knew their intent had been to do Ryan harm. At that point, my husband realised just how serious things were getting. All his anger and frustrations surfaced and he ran out after them and chased them down the road. He shouted that he knew who they were and would be reporting to their parents. Unfortunately, whilst I shared his anger, showing our feelings opened the flood gates.

From then on life was hell. Ryan's bedroom was at the front of the house, and day after day his windows were pelted with eggs and fruit and bottles. Huge gangs would stand outside and jeer and shout. If it wasn't so awful it would seem quite bizarre, because it wasn't just our son who was now the subject of bullying, but our whole family and our home, There would be about a dozen boys at least, shouting obscenities and hanging around outside. I felt really threatened and began to realise how Ryan must have felt. We told the Police, and the school, and the parents, but nothing stopped.

I moved Ryan into a back room where he could not hear what was going on, and I never told him about the phone calls. They started about a week after Halloween. First of all, there was just silence, then someone would ask for Ryan in a sing-song voice, then they started to call my husband names – probably because he was trying to stand up to them. It was intimidating and frightening and Ryan became a virtual prisoner in his own home because he was too scared to go outside. Apart from how Ryan felt, I was fearful for him, too. I could clearly see that it was not safe for him to go outside. If he were to meet any of them when he was on his own he wouldn't have stood a chance.

So that was how life was for a while. I took Ryan to school, he spent most of the day protecting himself, I collected him and we went home and he shut himself away in the back room. Two days a week he could relax with the other youngsters at Red Balloon, and then the routine would continue. He never went out alone, and on the occasions he joined me to walk the dog, jeering boys would miraculously appear and start taunting him. I would glare at them and guide Ryan away, but they were brazen and bold when there was more than one of them.

. I had even taped up the letterbox because I feared that something sinister might be put through, especially around Bonfire Night. Certainly fireworks were thrown at the windows and the house for weeks before and following November 5th. I knew if they ever had the opportunity they would throw one at Ryan.

I began to hate the place where we lived. We were trapped, and I was living in a constant state of expectation that something awful was going to happen. This was not the life I had wanted for my son. I longed for him to be outside in the summer sun, enjoying life like other children. He had done nothing wrong and had never hurt anyone. Things had spiralled out of control.

It was time to make a decision. Ryan could not continue hiding in his own home. Even my husband realised that drastic action had to be taken and that none of us could continue living as we were. We had changed the telephone number twice, hung thick net curtains at all the windows in the front of the house, and still they got to us. The phone calls continued until eventually I stopped answering the telephone.

Everything came to a head one morning. Ryan was complaining of stomach pains and was vomiting and I decided there and then that enough was enough. I sat beside Ryan and told him he was not going back to school and that he would be learning at home. I explained that I would buy all the coursework he needed, but that we would need a commitment from him to work hard and keep up to date with the work. The change in him was instantaneous. The sickness disappeared, he threw his school uniform in the cupboard, and he began smiling again. "I'll work so hard," he assured me, "thank you, mum," and he hugged me.

I had never felt such relief. We were finally doing something positive to resolve the ridiculous position we found ourselves in. No longer were we going to let these kids rule our lives. We were taking control.

I advised the authorities that Ryan was leaving the state education system and of course there were lots of letters back and forth from various government bodies telling us we would be closely monitored to ensure our son was being educated properly. Let them try. I was going to do whatever it took to ensure my son had as normal a life as possible.

The next step was to resign from my job. I fully intended that I would devote myself to providing the absolute best education I could for Ryan, and the only way I could do that was to give him my time. It meant vast changes financially, but there are times when you just have to do what has to be done.

I received a lot of condemnation not only from the teachers and school but also from some of our family. They could not understand why Ryan didn't just fight back. They thought I was crazy to give up work and the idea of home educating him was, in their eyes, ridiculous. But we were now determined that this was not how we were going to let Ryan live, and also we didn't want to stay in our home anymore. We wanted to live somewhere where we could all feel free to go outside whenever we wanted to without fear.

The next step was to find somewhere else to live and we put our house up for sale. I saw the look in other parents' eyes. They knew why we were moving, and I hoped they felt some guilt. We were determined to move as far away from the area as we could, and when we left on moving day we all cheered. We moved to a small village by the seaside where no-one knew us and nobody knew Ryan's story.

That was the turning point. As soon as Ryan was out of the threatening environment of school, he relaxed into his work. He settled into a routine of study and enjoyed the freedom to work without fear of intimidation. Whenever he chose he could walk outside and be on the beach and no-one followed him or called him names. He began to relax and realise that he could be free to go where he wished whenever he wanted.

It transpired that academically he was outstanding, and he obtained five GCSE's at age 14, studying set courses from a distance learning centre. He settled into a routine well and enjoyed the work. He was diligent and worked hard, determined that he was going to make the most of his abilities. He learned to be proud of his achievements as he gained high grades in his assignments, and gradually his self esteem and self belief grew. It was amazing and fantastic to see the change in him. He began to have confidence in his own abilities.

Our regime was strict. Work started at 9am until midday, then an hour for lunch, and then work would resume until about 3pm or later, depending on how much work he had to do. He thrived on routine. He knew what he had to do and how long he had to do it in, there was no outside distractions, his pencils and books would always be where he left them, and he always had me close by to discuss the work and to sound off ideas with. Sometimes if he was well ahead of schedule he would finish early and we would take the dog and walk on the beach. It was so wonderful to see him happy and relaxed.

Shortly after we had moved we began attending a local Baptist church, and Ryan decided he wanted to be baptised. It is the custom for the person being baptised to give a testimony. The church was packed full of people on the morning of the ceremony, and as Ryan went to the front of the church and adjusted the microphone I could see everyone smiling and expecting an amusing speech because he was known as a funny and likeable boy. He started his speech with 'I haven't had an easy life...' and I could see the surprise on the faces of the congregation. The fact that a 13-year-old looked back on his early years as a difficult time was really heart-breaking and it showed the effect that those years of emotional and physical abuse from his peers had had on him. He told his story from the heart, with no notes to refer to, just telling it as it was. At the end everyone was on their feet and applauding.

Getting his exams at fourteen meant that he had a year before he could go to Sixth Form College to study for A levels. During the time he was home educated he had become friendly with a group of other home educated children, as well as still keeping in touch with the kids from the Red Balloon centre. As his confidence grew so did his determination to get on in life, and he decided that he would like to take A levels at college. So whilst he was waiting to be old enough, he spent a year doing an Open University course. He didn't want to just sit back and take it easy, but he wanted to learn as much as he could.

He came to realise that he was a nice person who could form friendships, that he was gifted, and that he could achieve whatever he set his mind to. I would say that he still finds it difficult to trust people and it takes time for him to get to know people. I hope that as his confidence grows it will become easier. At Sixth Form college he was a straight A student who obtained an Outstanding Achievement Award two years running. He declined an offer of a place at one of the most prestigious Universities in the world, and in 2011 went to University to study Meteorology. I have no doubt in my mind whatsoever that if I had not made the decisions I made for Ryan he would not have developed into the sociable, intelligent and delightful young man that he is today. I urge all parents to take whatever steps you feel are necessary in order to give your child the best opportunity they can have. They only get one chance.

One of the assignments in Ryan's GCSE work was to write a story of a personal experience. It is to his credit that he chose to write about bullying, and his story follows.

Ryan's Story

I don't know why they always picked on me. All I ever wanted was to be part of the gang. For some reason I didn't fit in, and they made my life a misery.

How I longed to eat my lunch in the cafeteria with everyone else. Yet I also loathed the idea. I yearned for acceptance when it would not come; although when it did, it was a false impression. School had never been an easy ride, at some points it felt as though the roller coaster had derailed altogether. There were highs and lows, twists and turns, yet the ride never got any more enjoyable. I felt as though the world was against me most days. Even trying to establish a friendly conversation was near to impossible. So for now, I stayed on the stairs, away from everyone else, impossibly isolated.

I had a few acquaintances, yet they never seemed to have the time to eat with me, chattering and gossiping with their real friends. I felt as though nobody saw me, I was a ghost in their sight as they walked on by, not caring to stop and say hi. I never kept to the same place just in case they found me and started the taunting again just because I existed. I would sneak from stairwell to stairwell always on the move. I didn't always keep to the stairs and desolate corners; benches, empty classrooms, even, on occasions, teachers' offices just to get away from them.

Even getting to classes was an arduous and tricky task. I had to, of course, but I needed to keep myself concealed just in case they were right around the corner, or waiting around that bend with the threats, ridicule and jibes that left me with a feeling of utter hopelessness. If they did catch me I would be punched or kicked, tripped up or poked (like I had a choice!). I tried many tactics, from humouring them to trying to fight back, but I couldn't find the harshness of words, so it was to no avail. I just had to ignore it. But how can you ignore something so malicious and so repetitive, with the intent of causing as much misery as humanly possible. You can't. Simple as that. You try, but it all comes flooding back to you at the worst possible moment. So there was no other option but to keep hidden.

Classrooms were no escape from the heartless mockery. Every time I looked around people stared and giggled or handed me another note, most of which I tossed in the trash despite the fact I knew they were not even worthy of that. The ones I did read usually contained distasteful anecdotes of abuse. If I didn't read them, the flavourless drawings and words would magically transfer to my workbook. I would never let anyone borrow a pen as I knew there was a slim chance of ever getting it back again (and it would probably be used to scribble another note). Sometimes I thought it selfish keeping my equipment under such permanent guard.

At home there was no break from the intimidation. Objects were pelted at my bedroom window with no remorse. It felt as though they were beating my heart as well as my house. My curtains were kept closed; I was cocooned in my own world, and I was too frightened to leave that safe haven.

It seemed to me there was no other option. This was it. This was my school-life. I was destined to be a continuous joke in the eyes of my classmates. I had to get used to the idea of standing out, of being different. It made me feel so low sometimes I just gave up trying. I was walked over like a doormat, and treated like the dirt you'd find on it. I wouldn't bother greeting anyone as I walked past, they never greeted me, so what was the point? Why bother being friendly, I thought, it's not getting me anywhere! So I acted as I thought necessary. In lessons I didn't bother putting my hand up, even when I knew the answer for certain. I left it to the brainiac bullies to get the answer wrong. I wouldn't bother making conversation; I ate my lunch in silence, staring at a brick wall. After school my heart relaxed as I gave a sigh of relief. I hurried out before anyone else, desperate not to walk with anyone. Was this it? Was I going to have to act like this every day of my life?

So I started reviewing my options. Firstly, and most significantly, I left school completely. For the first few weeks I questioned myself, was this too drastic? Was I overreacting? Was my time really that bad? Secretly I knew all the answers to these questions, although I felt a bit of a chicken just dropping out like that. There must be other answers. Maybe I could go into school with a mean-looking rottweiler; nobody would dare even ponder crossing me then! But deep in my heart I knew I didn't belong there. So I started going to a new centre for bullied children. The environment was warm and friendly, and this wasn't the forced friendliness you would find in a busy school where the teachers crave a break, this was genuine.

The kids there totally understood what I went through, and many of them had had worse experiences than I had. All the sessions were confidence building and made me and many others believe in themselves again and find ways to beat the bullies in the process. I established many friendships and learned many skills to deal with my emotions. I was quite content. I would have happily carried on there were it not for a sudden decision to relocate to the coast.

I had finally got my ticket out of the village of the damned! We moved to a picturesque little community with the sea lapping at our door. It was probably one of the best decisions that we'd ever made. I said bon voyage to the fruit-stained windows and started afresh. Being next to the ocean was a great privilege. For Dibley, our labrador, it was truly heaven. For the first couple of months he would hide up as he had so many walks! Dad was often so eager he got up at 4am just to get down the beach! Life seemed so much more relaxed, and the village was warm and welcoming. Often if you greeted anyone with "Good morning!" where we used to live, you would receive a look of disdain and dismissal, whereas here the neighbours politely smile and respond. I was home

The only major sacrifice was leaving the centre, which took some time to get over, but there were other options, there were always other options. I was adamant not to return to mainstream school and determined to find a new busy social life, two things that are difficult to balance out. So there was one option left, home education.

The name conjured up a stereotypical image of a child imprisoned in their own home not allowed to associate with anyone or enjoy anything remotely fun whilst undergoing a military-like regime. This didn't exactly fill me with optimism! The first few weeks were daunting. It felt like playing a constant game of Tetris, once one piece of coursework was finished and filed another five came along and each one had to be completed and organised within a time limit. Needless to say, my "office" was getting pretty messy! At some points I just couldn't keep my concentration fiddling with anything I could reach, gazing out the window, whistling random tunes, anything to pass the time (especially when it came down to algebra!). However, in the coming weeks and months I got used to it and settled into the routine. I really hate to say it, but some of the work was kind of fun! Most importantly of all, I didn't have to keep continuously looking over my shoulder.

Then came the task of building a stable social life. This proved to be not as hard as I thought it would be. I joined a club for home educated children and found there was a surprising number in my area. We soon all made friends, and now I am enjoying many and varied friendships.

Now those days of constantly watching my back are but a distant memory and I'm living life to the full. I've already had my first real relationship with another home-educated girl. It lasted well, although I've learnt not to be so over-eager! I have a wide circle of supportive friends who always have my back when I need them. Now I'm laid back and don't care about other people's opinions. They don't matter. As far as I'm concerned they can think what they like, as long as I am happy with myself that's all that matters. To the losers who judged me and laughed in my face I say this, I've had the last laugh and I will become successful, no matter what it takes.

Update – Five Years On

I am writing this having just finished reading this book, five years after we wrote Freedom. I would like to document the changes that have occurred since that time, and how my life has dramatically opened up to a world of opportunity.

At the time of writing, I was in the process of completing my GCSE exams and applying for Sixth-Form College. I knew I had given my absolute best effort to the exams, but secretly expected mediocre results, not really believing I had the ability to achieve the top grades. Upon receiving my certificates, I was astounded to see only As and Bs, so much so I questioned several times (half-jokingly, but only half) whether my paper had been mixed up with a better student. My internal confidence in my abilities skyrocketed, but I maintained humbleness when receiving praise from friends and family.

From this I was accepted into college, where the real healing process began. Slowly I began to demolish the barriers I had built up over many years. The whole environment seemed to emanate positivity. I always maintained that people at school were there against their will, but people at college wanted to be there, to learn and achieve. Gradually I realised that the people who had once made life impossible were not there. I still found some aspects of socializing challenging. Because I initially hung back from forming relationships with complete strangers, it took time to integrate myself into college life. I still ate alone often, either in the mobile surfing the internet or in a classroom with others chatting in their cliques. After the first year, I realised that there was nobody to hide from. I began talking more to the people in my class and establishing stronger, more trusting relationships. The confidence gained from these few relationships played a major part in the next major step in my life: university.

The concept of independent living had initially seemed daunting, as I'm sure it did for most people. The idea of being responsible for my own choices, my diet, my safety, my choice of friends was a bit scary. Despite all this, I was determined to pursue my dream of weather forecasting, and applied for the Meteorology and Oceanography course at UEA. I never expected such an amazing experience!

From fresher's week, people seemed interested in me, my life and my interests. This was a completely foreign concept to me. I was also able to develop an interest in their lives and the things we had in common. I never expected people to be so open, so accepting and so supportive. Within weeks I was so overwhelmed with social activity it was a challenge to keep up with the work. I almost considered reserving my own bar stool at the Union Pub!

I became particularly close to one of the guys I met at a bible study group. It was one night when walking home from a pub that I found myself confiding in him my deepest secrets not even my parents knew. This was in stark contrast to the days I could not tell my own Mother about the bruises on my legs. I surprised myself at how comfortable and open I felt with him. From that point we developed a close, trusting friendship. I know I can tell him anything and he will not judge me, and vice versa. Without his continual support through the ever oscillating highs and lows of university life, I doubt I would have continued in education. If he is reading this, I hope he realizes just how significant that support has been.

Character traits that were perceived as weaknesses at school, and resultantly targeted, had the opposite effect at university. People respected my gentle nature, and used it to come to me with their problems and worries. I often joked about being the local agony aunt, but it felt so uplifting helping others with their problems considering the problems I faced in the past. I was pleasantly surprised to hear people telling me I was a "funny" or "likeable" guy, again, stark contrast to some of the names I have been called in the past.

The first year ended with an average exam score of 76%, a secure first class grade. Even this year I have noticed a significant growth in my confidence. I joined groups such as English Corner, a group which meets weekly to chat to international students and help them to practice English. From this I have become more extravert, meeting others who are feeling lonely and alienated in a new and strange country. It's so encouraging to see them form new friendships.

Early in 2013, I was forced to take a year off university for medical reasons. I took advantage of this to get back in contact with Red Balloon, the group that helped me many years ago when I was in a very dark place. Without them, I undoubtedly would not be where I am today, and dread to think where I could have been. I intended to volunteer at the centre, giving back my time to an organization to whom I may owe my life. It was astounding to see how quickly the group had developed. Now a full time school, students receive a personal, flexible education plan suited to their interests. This gives them opportunities that they never got in mainstream school where they were never allowed to reach their full potential. Here they can learn without fear, without watching their backs and without negative criticism. I was encouraged to see so many smiling faces full of promise. I volunteer in classes such as mathematics, science and PSHE, aiding and encouraging the students in their work. I hope Red Balloon realise the significance of what they have done in my life, and am sure they are doing the same for the lives of their current students.

Last but by no means least I would like to thank my parents for their support through all of this. I was not fully aware of how much they had done for me, what they had given up, the stress of making huge, rash decisions and the emotional trauma they themselves experienced. I truly owe them everything, and I hope they realize how grateful I am for that.

The future is looking bright with many areas of employment open to me. I still occasionally have problems with confidence in social situations and self-esteem, but these are negligible compared to the situation I was in when I first walked through the doors of the Red Balloon support center. The days of being too afraid to leave the house are over, I have in fact travelled all over Europe and beyond since then, and have no plans to stop travelling in the future. The people who made me queasy each morning are long forgotten. I cannot even remember some of the incidents mentioned in this book. The brain has been known to forget particularly painful memories. I don't care. I do not wish to remember, only to look forward in expectation. I had the last laugh, and have been laughing ever since.

AND FINALLY...

Ryan's story had a happy ending, but this is not always the case. Shortly after writing the above story, Ryan came across a website that encouraged youngsters to post their stories of things that had happened to them and the ways they had overcome them. He posted his story, and one of the comments from a reader was *'I'm fed up with hearing about bullying in school, it's all you ever hear about these days. You need to toughen up and get on with it'*. The comment was from a parent. Yes, there are a lot of reports of school bullying, and perhaps some people don't empathise with it. All I can say is that if I had not taken things into my own hands and fought for my son, I do not know what sort of person he would be today. He could have ended up hospitalised, on medication, even become suicidal. If there hadn't been that knock on the door when he was seven, I might never have gone down the path of finding out what was going on and doing something about it.

If I had a second chance, I would do it all over again. If we are supportive parents and want the best for our children, then we have to do whatever it takes. Don't worry about being a social outcast or bucking the system, make sure you are heard and that you get all the help and advice that you need to make life the best that it can be for your child.

HIDING

Always hiding,
Like a hunting cat,
Not with the purpose of taking a life,
But with preserving one.

Seeking new places
Not yet discovered
Becomes the secret goal,
Of every day.

The game of hide and seek
Makes blood run like clotting jelly
And the slightest breath
A howl of the wind.

How small the cupboard
In which the hunted hides,
As the walls fold inward
And the muffled sounds from beyond, tease.

Blackened bruises
With ragged edges,
Reminds the hunted
What awaits outside.

Toes curl in tight shoes
And watery eyes strain to see
What else lies hidden
In the darkness that is all around.

Musty air,
Cleaning cloths and dust
Offer reassurance
And security.

A handkerchief,
Hastily unfolded,
Mops a dripping nose
And an escaped tear.

Hushed whispers
Make the sweat flow
Slowly down the spine,
Like spittle on Grandma's chin.

The handle of the door
Turns like a giant wheel,
And the creak of hinges
Is the final sound of discovery.

Jane Finch

List of UK anti-bullying organisations in the UK:-

Kidscape.org.uk - useful resources for parents and young people affected by bullying including anti-bullying workshops. A registered *UK charity* committed to keeping children safe from harm or abuse.

Childline.org.uk – someone to talk to. 24/7 manned telephones. You don't have to face it alone. Contact ChildLine 24/7 for help.

Standagainstviolence.co.uk/bullying – anti-violence workshops. Make A Stand Against Violence Now. Think 2x Before You Act · Powerful PSHE Workshops · Anti-Violence Workshops

Kidpower.org – skills to stop bullying at school. Actions both children and adults can take.

Bullying.co.uk – advice regarding cyberbullying and bullying at work, bullying in school and general advice. Bullying advice from Bullying *UK* - bullying at work, cyberbullying, and find out how to deal with it from bullying organisation Bullying *UK*, part of Family Lives

Ditchthelabel.org – resources and statistics and support. Bullying Support, Resources and Statistics from the Leading and Award Winning *Anti-Bullying Charity*.

Cybersmile.org - The Cybersmile Foundation is a multi-award winning *anti* cyberbullying non-profit *organization* in the U.S and as a registered *charity* in the *U.K*

Respectme.org.uk – information on cyberbullying, children's rights, and resources.

Redballoonlearner.org - Red Balloon supports young people who self-exclude from school and are missing education because of bullying or other trauma. They provide an academic and therapeutic programme to enable our students to get back on track and reconnect with society.

Reproduced by kind permission of CBS News.

The following is an excerpt from a report posted by Amanda Cochran of CBS News Eye on Parenting on 13th August 2010.

Anti-Bullying Summit Held for America's Kids

NEW YORK (CBS) The Department of Education held its first-ever anti-bullying summit on Wednesday and Thursday in Washington. The goal of the summit was to engage governmental and non-governmental partners in crafting a national strategy to reduce and end bullying. Education Secretary Arne Duncan opened the two-day summit Wednesday on the dangers of bullying inside and outside the classroom.

Bullying has long been an issue in schools, but in recent years - with the accessibility of texting and the Internet - the problem has grown. In fact, the issue of bullying garnered national attention after the deaths of students like 15-year-old Phoebe Prince of Massachusetts who took her own life last January allegedly in response to constant harassment and bullying from some of her classmates.

At the summit, Duncan and other panel participants spoke about the need to be vigilant in their schools and communities and address bullying if they see or hear about it.

But what can parents do to stop bullying behavior or detect if their child is being bullied?

CBS News Medical Correspondent Dr. Jennifer Ashton recommends parents look for these potential indicators in their child:

-Comes home with torn or damaged clothing or missing belongings

-Has unexplained cuts or bruises

-Seems afraid of going to school, riding the bus or participating in activities

-Drop in school grades

-Complains often of physical ailments

-Has trouble sleeping or loss of appetite.

Taken from **Loveourchildrenusa.org**

Bullying is one of the most minimized and persistent problems in our schools today. The sad thing is – it's a reality for all children, whether they're victims, witnesses, or they're the bullies.

Children are born into the world innocent – without defences. Another child or an adult comes along who is a product of abuse, rage, or being a 'bully' victim and the cycle continues. Whether it's at school or at home, anyone who is bullied will very often feel depressed and have low self-esteem. And if you're a bully, you are more likely to be hostile and antisocial. If you're a bully, who has been bullying you?

Do You Know What Bullying Is?

It's physical harm, it's verbal and emotional terrorism, it's sexual harassment, its racism .. and at times it can grow into much more serious abuse – and criminal behavior.

If someone is hitting, biting, kicking, punching, pinching you, pulling your hair, tripping you – that's physical bullying.

If someone is relentlessly teasing you, calling you names, spreading rumors about you, leaving you out of group activities – that's verbal and emotional terrorism.

If someone touches you inappropriately, snaps your bra strap, stares at your body, or makes sexual comments – that's sexual bullying.

If someone is using racial slurs against you, making fun of your customs, the color of your skin, your accent, or the food you eat, if they spray symbols and graffiti on your house, if they tease you about your country – that's racial bullying.

Bullying is when someone keeps doing or saying things to have power over another person.

Some of the ways they bully other people are by: calling them names, saying or writing nasty things about them, leaving them out of activities, not talking to them, threatening them, making them feel uncomfortable or scared, taking or damaging their things, hitting or kicking them, or making them do things they don't want to do.

Have any of these things happened to you? Have you done any of these things to someone else? Bullying is wrong behavior which makes the person being bullied feel afraid or uncomfortable.

Understanding Bullying

If you understand bullying, you can help to stop it.

A bully just doesn't become a bully and they're not born that way. A bully is usually being bullied or abused at home. They usually have low self-esteem which they got by being a victim. Bullying is learned behavior, and what's learned can be unlearned. They don't have to continue the cycle.

There are a lot of reasons why some people bully.

They may see it as a way of being popular, or making themselves look tough and in charge. Some bullies do it to get attention or things, or to make other people afraid of them. Others might be jealous of the person they are bullying. They may be a victim of being bullied themselves.

Some bullies may not even understand how wrong their behavior is and how it makes the person being bullied feel.

If a kid is being bullied, they will pick on other kids because it's the only thing they know and it's a way of dealing with it. Bullying makes them feel powerful. They have a special need to feel popular – because they're never praised at home. The bully is really insecure, but they'll never let you see that side of them. They'll go after someone weaker, smaller, and different. They'll take away your self-esteem and scare you.

Bullying Is Harmful

Some people think bullying is just part of growing up and a way for young people to learn to stick up for themselves. But bullying can make young people feel lonely, unhappy and frightened. It makes them feel unsafe and think there must be something wrong with them. They lose confidence and may not want to go to school any more. It may make them sick.

Are You Being Bullied? Here's How You Can Stop It!

Coping with bullying can be difficult, but remember, you are not the problem, the bully is. You have a right to feel safe and secure.

If you're different in some way, be proud of it! Stand strong. Spend time with your friends - bullies hardly ever pick on people if they're with others in a group.

You've probably already tried ignoring the bully, telling them to stop and walking away whenever the bullying starts. If someone is bullying you, you should always tell an adult you can trust. This isn't telling tales. You have a right to be safe and adults can do things to get the bullying stopped.

Even if you think you've solved the problem on your own, tell an adult anyway, in case it happens again.

An adult you can trust might be a teacher, school principal, parent, someone from your family or a friend's parent. If you find it difficult to talk about being bullied, you might find it easier to write down what's been happening to you and give it to an adult you trust.

What Can You Do If You See Someone Else Being Bullied?

If you see someone else being bullied, you should always try to stop it. If you do nothing, you're saying that bullying is okay with you.

Treat others the way you would like to be treated. Show the bully that you think what they're doing is stupid and mean. Help the person being bullied to tell an adult they can trust.

Are You A Bully?

Have you ever bullied someone? Think about why you did it and how you were feeling at the time. If you are sometimes a bully, try to find other ways to make yourself feel good.

Most bullies aren't liked, even if it starts out that way. Remember … treat others the way you would like to be treated.

Get Help

Teachers and parents have a special responsibility for looking after kids – especially helping you if you're being bullied at school. It's not so easy to identify a bully. Is the bully really being hostile and aggressive toward you or are they just having what they call 'fun?'

When someone is bullied at school, your friends and acquaintances usually know what is going on. Even though they're not involved they know it's happening. Adults can't always tell and need your help in order to help you or your friends.

All members of a school community — whether they're kids or teachers, have a responsibility to help kids who are being bullied. You and your friends must speak out against the bullies.

* Nobody has the right to hurt anyone else by hitting them, calling then names or doing anything which is hurtful.
* Bullying is wrong – no matter how old you are.
* If an adult is bullying you or trying to make you do something you think is wrong, it is imperative that you tell someone immediately.

Help Your Friends

You can help other kids who are being bullied. Encourage them to talk to an adult, or offer to talk to an adult on their behalf. You might be able to let bullies know that you do not like what they are doing and that you are determined to stop them. Be empowered. Tell the bully you don't like what they're doing to your friends. Walk away. Don't give in to their threats or challenges..

All profits from the sale of this book will be donated to Red Balloon Learner Centres.

Red Balloon Learner Centres,

7a Chesterton Mill

French's Road, Cambridge

CB4 3NP, England

Tel: 01223 366052

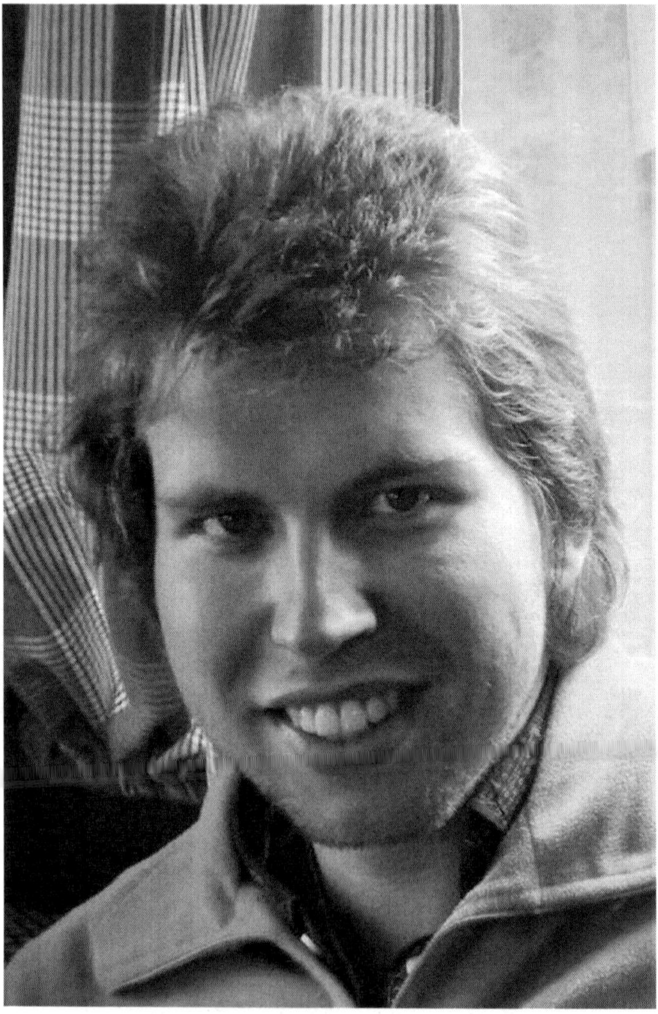

16553391R00058

Printed in Great Britain
by Amazon